Ladybird
Action Rhymes

Action
songs

compiled by Helen Finnigan
illustrated by Roger Langton

d Books

One finger, one thumb keep moving,
One finger, one thumb keep moving,
One finger, one thumb keep moving,
We'll all be merry and bright.

One finger, one thumb, one arm,
    keep moving,
One finger, one thumb, one arm,
    keep moving,
One finger, one thumb, one arm,
    keep moving,
We'll all be merry and bright.

One finger, one thumb, one arm, *one leg*,
    keep moving, *etc*.

One finger, one thumb, one arm, one leg,
    one nod of the head, keep moving, *etc*.

The rhyme may be continued with other verses –
stand up, sit down, turn round, *etc*.

4

Contents

British Library Cataloguing in Publication Data

Action songs
1. Children's action songs in English. Words – Anthologies
I. Finnigan, Helen   II. Langton, Roger
784.6'2405
ISBN 0-7214-1166-5

First edition

Published by Ladybird Books Ltd Loughborough Leicestershire UK
Ladybird Books Inc Auburn Maine 04210 USA

Row, row, row your boat,
Gently down the stream.
Merrily, merrily, merrily, merrily,
Life is but a dream.

If you're happy and you know it,
Clap your hands.
If you're happy and you know it,
Clap your hands.
If you're happy and you know it,
Then you surely want to show it,
If you're happy and you know it,
Clap your hands.

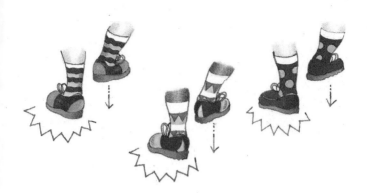

If you're happy and you know it,
Nod your head, *etc*.

If you're happy and you know it,
Stamp your feet, *etc*.

If you're happy and you know it,
say "ha, ha!"

If you're happy and you know it, do all four!

7

Old McDonald had a farm
E...I...E...I...O
And on that farm he had some cows,
E...I...E...I...O
With a moo-moo here,
And a moo-moo there,
Here a moo, there a moo,
Everywhere a moo-moo,
Old McDonald had a farm,
E...I...E...I...O

Old McDonald had a farm,
E...I...E...I...O
And on that farm he had some ducks,
E...I...E...I...O
With a quack-quack here,...*etc.*

...*cats*...mew-mew...

...*horses*...neigh-neigh...

...*dogs*...woof-woof...

...*lambs*...baa-baa...

8

Moo moo

Adjust the speed of this song to suit the age of the child; older children can be encouraged to memorise what has gone before

e.g. 'with a quack-quack here,
And a quack-quack there,
Here a quack, there a quack,
Everywhere a quack-quack,
Moo-moo here, moo-moo there,' *etc.*

9

Sing a song of sixpence,
A pocket full of rye;
Four and twenty blackbirds
Baked in a pie!
When the pie was opened
The birds began to sing;
Wasn't that a dainty dish
To set before the king?

The king was in his counting house,
Counting out his money;

The queen was in the parlour,
Eating bread and honey.

The maid was in the garden,
Hanging out the clothes,

When down came a blackbird
And pecked off her nose.

The train is a-coming, oh yes,
Train is a-coming, oh yes,
Train is a-coming, train is a-coming,
Train is a-coming, oh yes.

You'd better get your ticket, oh yes,
Better get your ticket, oh yes,
Better get your ticket, better get your ticket,
Better get your ticket, oh yes.

There's room for a few more, oh yes, *etc*.

The train is a-leaving, oh yes, *etc*.

We're going to the seaside, oh yes, *etc*.

We've got to go home now, oh yes, *etc*.

13

There was a princess long ago,
Long ago, long ago,
There was a princess long ago,
Long ago.

And she lived in a big high tower, *etc*.

One day a fairy waved her wand, *etc*.

The princess slept for a hundred years, *etc*.

A great big forest grew around, *etc.*

A gallant prince came riding by, *etc.*

He took his sword and cut it down, *etc.*

He took her hand to wake her up, *etc.*

So everybody's happy now, *etc.*

Leader: I am a music man,
I come from far away,
And I can play.

All: What can you play?

Leader: I play piano.

All: Pia, pia, piano, piano, piano,
Pia, pia, piano, pia, piano.

Leader: I am a music man,
I come from far away,
And I can play.

All: What can you play?

Leader: I play the big drum.

All: Boomdi, boomdi, boomdi boom,
Boomdi boom, boomdi boom,
Boomdi, boomdi, boomdi boom,
Boomdi, boomdi boom,
Pia, pia, piano, piano, piano,
Pia, pia, piano, pia, piano.

Leader: I am a music man,
I come from far away,
And I can play.

All: What can you play?

Leader: I play the trumpet.

All: Tooti, tooti, tooti, toot,
Tooti, toot, tooti, toot,
Tooti, tooti, tooti, toot,
Tooti, tooti, toot.
Boomdi, boomdi, boomdi boom,
Boomdi boom, boomdi boom,
Boomdi, boomdi, boomdi boom,
Boomdi, boomdi boom,
Pia, pia, piano, piano, piano,
Pia, pia, piano, pia, piano.

Do your ears hang low?
Do they wobble to and fro?

Can you tie them in a knot?
Can you tie them in a bow?
Can you toss them over your shoulder
Like a regimental soldier?
Do your ears hang low?

Yankee Doodle came to town
Upon a little pony;
He stuck a feather in his cap
And called it macaroni.

Chorus (to follow each verse)
Yankee doodle, doodle do,
Yankee doodle dandy;
All the lasses are so smart,
And sweet as sugar candy.

First he bought a porridge pot,
Then he bought a ladle,
Then he trotted home again
As fast as he was able.

Marching in and marching out,
And marching round the town O;
Here comes a regiment
With Captain Thomas Brown O.

Yankee Doodle is a tune,
That comes in mighty handy,
The enemy all runs away
At Yankee Doodle Dandy.

John Brown's baby
got a cold
upon his chest,

  John Brown's baby
got a cold
upon his chest,

John Brown's baby
got a cold
upon his chest,

So they rubbed it with camphorated oil,
Camphor-amphor-amphor-ated,
Camphor-amphor-amphor-ated,
Camphor-amphor-amphor-ated,
So they rubbed it with camphorated oil.

Hot Cross Buns, Hot Cross Buns,

One a penny, two a penny,
Hot Cross Buns.

If you have no daughters,
Give them to your sons,
One a penny, two a penny,
Hot Cross Buns.

Jump, jump, jump if you feel you want to,
Jump, jump, jump if you feel you can,
Jump, jump, jump if you feel you want to,
Jump, jump, jump if you feel you can.

Jump, jump, jump if you're feeling happy,
Jump, jump, jump if you feel you can,
Jump, jump, jump if you feel you want to,
Jump, jump, jump if you feel you can.

Dance, dance, dance when you hear
    a band play,
Sing, sing, sing when you hear a tune,
Skip, skip, skip when you're feeling ropy,
Clap, clap, clap all together now.

Laugh, laugh, laugh if you're only joking,
Laugh, laugh, laugh if you're having fun,
Laugh, laugh, laugh when you have
    a good time,
Laugh, laugh, laugh and we'll all join in.

She'll be coming round the mountain
    when she comes,
She'll be coming round the mountain
    when she comes,
She'll be coming round the mountain,
Coming round the mountain,
Coming round the mountain,
    when she comes.

Chorus (to follow each verse)
Singing, aye, aye, ippy, ippy, aye,
Singing, aye, aye, ippy, ippy, aye,
Singing, aye, aye, ippy,
Aye, aye, ippy,
Aye, aye, ippy, ippy, aye.

She'll be driving six white horses, *etc.*

Oh we'll all go out and meet her, *etc.*

She'll be wearing pink pyjamas, *etc.*

Oh she'll have to sleep with Grandma, *etc.*

In Dublin's fair city, where the girls
 are so pretty,
I first set my eyes on sweet Molly Malone,

As she wheeled her wheelbarrow,
Through streets, broad and narrow,

Crying "cockles and mussels, a-live,
 a-live oh!"

Chorus (to follow each verse)
A-live, a-live oh!
A-live, a-live oh!
Crying cockles and mussels,
A-live, a-live oh!

She was a fishmonger, but sure
    'twas no wonder,
For so were her father and mother before,
And they each wheeled their barrow,
Through streets, broad and narrow,
Crying "cockles and mussels, a-live,
    a-live oh!"

Chorus

She died of a fever and no one could
    save her,
And that was the end of sweet Molly Malone.
Her ghost wheels her barrow,
Through streets, broad and narrow,
Crying "cockles and mussels, a-live,
    a-live oh!"

Chorus